PAIN:
THE ACCELERATOR TO
A LIFE OF PURPOSE

MELODY KASHUMBA

PAIN: The Accelerator To A Life of Purpose

ISBN: 978-0-578-85220-1

Author: Melody Kashumba
Editor: Valerie L. McDowell
Cover Design: Daniel O. Ojedokun
Publisher: Power2Excel

Printed In The United States

PAIN:
THE ACCELERATOR TO
A LIFE OF PURPOSE

MELODY KASHUMBA

DEDICATION I

To My Children,

Taking a moment to give all praise and honor to the most-high God who through his Son, the Anointed Jesus Christ of Nazareth, graced me the power to write my journey of moving in the direction of the fire that burns within.

I would like to express extreme gratitude to my three precious children - Onari, Mudiwa and Shanti - who light up my world and motivate me to keep pressing in. My children have been with me through the fire and by the grace of God they are all coming out on top.

May God continue to open immeasurable doors for you my blessed children.

DEDICATION II

To My Family, Loved Ones and Destiny Helpers,

Love and Grace to my family - my Mom, Dad and my brothers and sisters - our family of five who are the real cast members in the story of my life. We made our own family history and changed our generation. I love you family and thank you for allowing me to be a part of our amazing legacy of excellence.

To my family in the four corners of the world, thank you!

I thank everyone who has been a part of my journey. There are too many names to mention.

To those who spoke life into my journey, prophesied the book before it ever came to be and accepted me as I am.

To the amazing women and men of impact I have had the privilege to encounter, I say thank you! I thank you and am deeply humbled to know you.

May this book bring Glory to our God and reveal his power and strength through the Anointed Jesus Christ of Nazareth.

A FATHER'S BLESSING

*The title of the book, PAIN: The Accelerator To A Life of Purpose,
is an all-encompassing book, involving people of various ages, religions,
ethnicities, and genders. What the world will be eagerly waiting to
hear from the book will be the texture and format of PURPOSE!
People will read and see the strategic elements of time, gender,
environment, education, and ethnicity, and how these attributes are
strategic to achieving a purpose, if properly implemented!*

*I am not surprised by your mental capability, nor that you have
joined enlightened groups, for you are exceedingly overwhelming in
intellectual output! You have signaled our realistic direction in life,
the direction of robust mental health and material and
spiritual blessings!*

*May God continue to bless you daughter, a key family figure in faith,
in God, and in confronting illiteracy and ethnic poverty!*

CONTENTS

FOREWORD

From the moment that I connected with Melody Kashumba some three years ago before she started writing her book, I was immediately struck by her gentle spirit; humility and love that easily oozes out of her. Every time you speak with her, you get to connect to the grace of God that is operating in her life. After you get to hear of all that she has gone through, you begin to understand that only God could have spiritually empowered her to embrace the bad hand that life had dealt her.

When I first got hold of the manuscript of the book, **PAIN: The Accelerator To A Life of Purpose,** I could not stop the tears from streaming down my cheeks. As a pain survivor myself, I immediately connected to the anguish embedded in the title and the hope that was ignited in me as I understood how Melody had turned her pain into gain. Gain not only for herself, but for all the women out there who need to understand how to *"navigate through those seasons of pain and hardship and use them to birth their transformation to a whole new level."*

The tears of joy quickly turned into shouts of victory and thanksgiving to God as scripture was being fulfilled in my own eyes. What the devil had made for bad; God had turned around for good. What should have killed Melody was now her steppingstone to something greater than the sum of all the pain that she had gone through.

It was noticeably clear that all the pain she had gone through from her early childhood, living in and leaving Zimbabwe up to the time she went to America was channeling and directing her to her purpose. If I were to use a four-letter word to describe her anguish; that word would be PAIN. It is unfortunate that a lot of people go through pain without ever coming to a revelation that pain is not an end in itself; pain is what propels you to your purpose and destiny.

If Melody were a student in the University of Pain, she would have earned herself a Doctorate and would have been on her way to becoming a Professor of Pain.

The bible says in Romans 8:28 that all things work together for good for those who love the Lord and are called according to his purposes. This means that loss, bereavement, sickness, bankruptcy, rejection, divorce, accusations, stress, etc. are all used by God to fuel you and channel you in the direction of your purpose. Nothing is wasted. These negative situations act as a fuel which ignites a fire and a passion inside you that acts as a force that propels you to a place you would never have gone to, had you not experienced any pain.

Without the betrayals, the divorce, raising a child with challenges in America and financial problems, Melody would not have been inspired or driven to come up with this book.

In my view, this is a must have book for women who are going through cyclical seasons of pain and are living their lives as victims of life circumstances. They have resorted to worldly solutions such as alcohol and drugs to give them temporary relief, when what they need is an understanding of how pain is an accelerator to purpose.

An accelerator in a car controls the speed of the car, the more pressure you apply on the paddle, the faster the car goes. The same can be said of pain. The more pain your experience, the closer you are to being drawn to your purpose. In other words, the intensification of pain is an indication of the "acceleration" of the pace that you are cruising at to get to your destiny.

After you read this book, you will be able to embrace your pain and allow it to help you step into your purpose. See you on the other side of pain.

Dr. Abigail Magwenzi, the author of *The Red Lipstick Stays On: You Don't Have to Look Like What You Are Going Through*! She is the Editor-In-Chief of the Red Lipstick Business Magazine and Commander-In-Chief of the Red Lipstick Revolution.

INTRODUCTION

Pain and hardship. Two things in which women are intimately familiar. But woven deep within the pain and hardship lie hidden potential, increased capacity, and great influence. But keep in mind, pain comes to ignite the greatness inside. Women who have been through cycles of pain are marked for greatness with that pain often being a smokescreen blinding them from their destiny. Yet when a woman becomes aware that the pain in her life is standing between her and her greatness, she is like a lit fuse, suddenly ignited, and fighting back to stand resolutely on top of the pain, reveling in her authentic value.

This book is written to help women navigate through seasons of pain and hardship, using those seasons to birth their transformation to a whole new level. But she must first have the right perspective and tools, or the pain can become paralyzing. But with the right tools, and with the awareness of the reason for their pain, it is no longer a hindrance but can be converted to fuel, accelerating these women into their next season.

Moving women from paralyzing pain to purpose is the message I am sent to convey. Moving in the direction of destiny includes navigating different seasons and moving towards a force that is pulling you. It is a steady pace, chasing purpose from seed time to harvest and manifestation.

This book chronicles my journey of chasing the fire that burns on the inside, birthed through life experiences. Each life experience was another piece of wood that was needed to set up the base of the fire, and once ignited, purpose would birth a life of no limits.

Chapter 1

PAINFUL ENCOUNTERS

When I was in primary school, which is considered elementary and middle school in the United States of America, I distinctly remember being bullied by a young lady whose face I can still see clear as day. For some reason, out of all the other girls at school, she singled me out, and would physically hit me, all while a crowd of students stood cheering. Looking back, no one ever stepped up or stood up for me, including my peers, schoolteachers, or passersby. This event happened at the end of the school year. Prior to that time, she would seek me out and constantly tell me that "today was the day" she was going to hit me. This occurred every three months like clockwork, just before we went off for our quarterly holiday. And I remember a crowd would follow us to a grass clearing as she declared it was "Closing Day." It was at this clearing that I would be stripped of any trace of power, hope, and joy.

As soon as she was done with what she deemed her assignment to strip me of my power, people would simply disperse and go on with their day as if nothing had happened. It would take me a while to see through the force exerted by her hands as she "double-clapped" both my cheeks simultaneously. I remember peering through the tears after the fact, looking at the people laughing, visibly enjoying the moment, as if it were some sporting event. It was hard to comprehend, but they were enjoying my pain. This would become a log of wood strategically placed in my soul.

I was alone.

I remember going home, but I did not tell anyone what had happened. I remember crying, my face burning. I also clearly remember the feeling of betrayal and mocking. I sat there paralyzed and confused as to why I was the recipient of such hostility. Interestingly, the one thing that stood out to me is that despite the pain, it did not take away from who I was. Even through the embarrassment, confusion, and pain, a controlled fire was beginning to ignite underneath. I could already begin to feel its quiet, hidden, yet steady strength brooding.

Chapter 2

PERCEPTION AND MINDSET

The dictionary defines perception as "the ability to see, hear, or become aware of something through the senses."

When I was a little girl, my family experienced times of having more than enough and times of not knowing if we would have food to eat or a place to stay. I remember coming home one day noticing my bed was out on the street. Without even asking, I knew we had been evicted. Even though for a time our family situation remained precarious, my father would often take us to Harare, Zimbabwe International Airport to watch the planes take off, allowing us to imagine, for just a moment, we were somewhere outside our norm. Whether he knew it or not, he was imparting in us a vision that there was more to life than where we currently stood. My father taught us to win the war of the mind and see beyond the clouds and smoke of the immediate environment. Through prayer and fasting, we tapped into a divine perception, the mind of Christ. Our family may have been lacking in the moment, but the promise was greater than the illusion.

One particular trip to the airport would forever become a life-changing encounter spring boarding me into a life of no limits. From my humble beginnings in my parents' home, I remember how relentless they were in trying to provide for our family of seven. The periods of plenty that were often followed by periods of lack included times with no electricity, transportation, or even close relationships. It was in these times that I can remember being a people watcher, hearing the opinions of people that did not appreciate my parents' vision of a life beyond the mundane. No matter the season we were in, my parents believed greater was coming. They lived every moment with gratitude, seizing every opportunity to look towards the future with hope. It is in one of these moments that I distinctly remember our numerous road trips to the airport. As we all piled into our current refurbished car, we would make our way, carrying some warm clothes with us, as we often would stay at the airport into the night. As I think back now, I wonder how we looked to those that saw us filing into the airport. That vision for me is still vivid to this day. As we walked into the airport, the electricity was so illuminating and beautiful. To this day, I love and appreciate electricity because there was a time this basic commodity was considered a luxury in my life.

We entered the airport, and on a large wall on my right, was a flattened golden-brown globe of the world. The globe was alive with mini lights showing each international destination where the planes would fly. All together, these little lights shined brightly, creating an unforgettable imprint on my mind, my soul, and my life. So many destinations, so many possibilities, and so much more beyond my humble life. It was clear there was more that my eyes could see in the world. We would confidently march through the airport and find ourselves in the waiting area where families congregated, waiting for their beloved ones. We would have small, treasured snacks, depending on the season of our life, feast, or famine. However, our hearts and minds were full of possibilities and dreams. I remember being surrounded by great wealth and influenced by the distinct smell of expensive scents lingering in the air; scents I attribute to international brands today. It was such a musical place for my senses; the sights, the smells, and the sounds – all colliding into a great symphony, pouring fuel into every cell of my body, and instilling within me a desire to chase a life of limitless possibilities, if I only believed.

And for me, I could believe it because I could see it. On the balcony, as the passengers disembarked to and from the different airlines like Qantas, an Australian Airline, British Airways, KLM the Royal Dutch Airlines, Ethiopian Airways, Air Zimbabwe, and Lufthansa German Airlines, I too, saw myself coming and going from all of these places as well. I was engulfed in all that was happening, even in all the cheering, welcome shouts, whistles, and cries. As the passengers took off, families cried, wailed, or cheered; it was quite an experience. We would find ourselves thick in the cheers, caught up in the moment, celebrating and empathetic with the families. The atmosphere was filled with emotion that could not be ignored.

We would go through this rehearsal over the years until I began to know that one day, I would be the one to walk on the tarmac, waving goodbye to my family. After all, I knew how many steps I would walk before I would look back, for I had seen it done so often. I would get to the airplane door one day, look back, and wave goodbye one last time to my family, as I pressed into my purpose, suspended in destiny.

This atmosphere continued as I grew up. I can still see myself in the various growth stages of my life at the airport, standing on the rails, then the bench, then standing on the ground. Eventually I would sit and meditate on when I was finally going to walk onto the plane. I waited in anticipation of that day.

Chapter 3

A LIFE IN PURPOSE: FROM ZIMBABWE TO THE WORLD

My very existence has been a journey for which I now see every intricate blending of many threads coming together. As early as eight years old, I remember standing on a mountaintop marveling at the possibilities before me. My mind would take pictures, make mental notes, and formulate dreams and visions. Anytime I would see something new, my territory and the world of possibilities expanded. As a child, I was curious, and I paid attention to my surroundings. I did not realize this curiosity would be taking impressions that would eventually direct me towards my passion and purpose.

In middle school in Africa, we would have international students visit from around the world. They would visit from different countries including Denmark, Australia, Netherlands, and Austria, to mention a few. As an introvert, I was always silently processing life and watching. Yes, these were those years I was bullied by the school bully with students jeering on. I never really had real girlfriends away from school. There was always a tendency to classify me as a friend until someone more interesting came or visited, then they would drop me for the day or for good.

During middle school, my family went through cycles of lack and abundance. High school was challenging as well since my parents often did not have the tuition funds to keep me in school. I remember the feeling when the school bursar would come into class to read aloud the names of people whose tuition was not paid. Yes, I was on the list, and after the bursar was done, we would have to pack our belongings and leave the premises. We were told to return when tuition was paid. Some of my peers knew their issue would be settled soon and they would be back to class. As I left school with tears running down my cheeks, I knew my case was different. I would be out for a while, and it was a gut-wrenching experience because I loved school. I knew education was my key to a better future. I remember sitting out of school so long that it became normal. But there was one time when I knew the tuition had been paid, but the receipts were lost, and the post office could not help until I had the right dates. Daily I would find my way into the city to the main post office to give them another day to look for my tuition receipt. Automation and technology did not exist during this period of the 90s. We had no way of automatically searching for the tuition receipt in the system. So, as I patiently endured this quest for the missing receipt, day in and day out, I ended up missing a whole chunk of high school at 14 years old.

At 15, I started working every holiday at my first job as an entertainment director, at a resort called Caribbea Bay. The job secured my school fees and required uniforms for the coming semester. My parents did all they could for the five of us, but this is my story. By the time I was 16, I pressed in intentionally and saved every penny I could and independently got a passport. I was compelled to start working towards the future.

I applied to several colleges, and in all honesty, I was not sure what I would study. During this time, many people from Zimbabwe were migrating to the United Kingdom and the United States. Nursing was a trend when you were in a foreign land. It provided lucrative compensation that would allow us to send money back home. Considering my background, it was important to pursue a career that would give me the ability to provide for my parents and family. I can only speak for myself when I say I thought that was the reason I chose nursing. However, what I would eventually learn was that nursing chose me. Many years later, I realized all the cycles of pain I went through in my life gave me deep compassion for my patients. I know how it is to feel emotional pain, mental pain, and yes, physical pain. I understand lonely nights, uncertainty, and above all, the difference compassion and love can make in an instant.

When deciding on where to study for college, I remembered a good friend from high school who had moved to Clearwater, Florida. In my search, it was an organic decision when the opportunity presented itself to join her. I knew it would be beneficial to have her guidance and help in transitioning. So that was my destination when I left Zimbabwe, Africa. I was on my way - out of my country, to another country, to Clearwater, Florida - in search of a different life. Every step I took to move to the United States, completing the required documents, arranging accommodations, connections, and the airplane ticket, were all by divine provision, even supernatural paths I believe. I was just a child with a fire that burned deep inside. I believed. I had faith and I stepped out in faith and began my move to the United States. God provided, doors opened, and I boldly stepped through them all.

Manifestation of the Process

It was in 1999 that God opened the door, and my destiny encounter arrived as I walked down the tarmac. After much scrimping and saving and praying and receiving the blessing of my family, my voyage to America to attend college on a visa had begun. When I got to the threshold, I waved goodbye to my family who were standing there, heaped on the too-familiar balcony. I waved and waved, then I continued to walk. There was one more stop. I walked up the stairs, tears pouring down my cheeks because I knew I was making history, writing a different story for my family, changing generational patterns, and would someday represent my country. The top of the stairs seemed still a distance away. As I soaked in the moment, I could feel my breath escaping me. I knew at 19 years of age that I may not see my family for a long time. However, I was aware that a pioneer does not have time to cry. I was going to new territory to discover, conquer, and call forth the rest.

Finally, I arrived at the last step and stopped as I had seen many international travelers do, standing at the door of Lufthansa Airlines, that familiar German Airline. I internally took a long, slow bow as the first chapter of my life in Zimbabwe, Africa was ending. It was clear that it was time for a new chapter, and this long metal object would be suspended in the air for close to 11 hours. After that, I would arrive at my destination; a new season would officially begin. Tears running down my face, this young girl lifted her hands and waved goodbye one last time. I can hear the wailing of my family and the shouts of my brothers calling my name through the piercing Zimbabwe air. At some point, flooded with tears, I made my way into the airplane, took a seat, and continued to wave through the window. The airline lifted off and I was alone. I was alone but not alone. I was full of purpose with a passion to be more, do more, see more. I was full of possibilities, moving in the direction of the fire inside.

I arrived in the United States of America and took a breath. It was everything I imagined and more. I saw palm trees for the first time. They were beautiful. Prior to my arrival, I consumed everything I could about Florida and the United States of America. I fed my mind pictures and videos from the American Information Center in Harare, Zimbabwe. Recalling these pictures, I saw my dream and reality collide so beautifully. There were neon lights in the signs as we drove from the airport, and the first stop was McDonald's. Amazing, exhilarating, and totally a miracle.

Chapter 4

HEROIC TAKE-OFF/ SOBERING START

When I left Africa, I was full of my pursuit, leaning into this force calling me to the United States of America. I would descend on American soil and be greeted by an old good friend. It's amazing how time changes people. After the initial euphoria of landing and seeing palm trees for the first time, seeing the neon signs on fast food restaurants, and McDonald's for the first time, and everything in America, reality set in; I would be living life in a first world country on a very slim budget. On arrival into America, it was truly a culture shock, to say the least. The first few days were a roller coaster trying to adjust to different time zones, preparing for school, and settling in. I tagged along with one of the friends of my friend, who was going to church the first week I arrived. I was deep in faith prior to coming to the United States so I was excited to be able to get connected to a church here in my new home. As we were all getting acquainted, another one of these newfound friends mentioned needing her hair done and I offered. During my years in Africa, I was often doing other people's hair and had learned to do my own hair well. I started doing her hair simply because I loved doing hair. I mention these incidents because they were significant. My steps from the time I arrived in the US were ordered by God. It was important to have developed a relationship with that first young lady by doing her hair because I needed to find uncommon favor with her. It was also important for me to find a connection with the friend I went to church with because I would need her kindness and mercy. I did not know this at the time. In humility, I had been sensitive to respond appropriately to these two women.

The Pain of Chasing Purpose

Less than a month into my arrival, my euphoric experience was cut short. Everything had been going well and my steps felt as if they were perfectly ordered by heaven above. However what life has taught me is that not all steps towards our destiny are without pain. Pain and adversity can appear, and they can also accelerate our growth, increase our capacity and even activate fire within us to push forward. My well put together start in the US shifted unexpectedly when my friend turned against me and my world changed overnight. She had received me, but suddenly her attitude towards me changed. She basically rescinded her hospitality in exchange for my eviction. She took all my belongings, and one by one, threw them outside the door of her apartment. As she was yelling at me, she told me I was "riff raff," worse than the dirt under her feet. According to Google, riff raff means *disreputable or undesirable people*. I was simply a young child with a dream, chasing that dream and entrusting my new life to an old friend. I was crying, tears pouring from my eyes, in what would become an all too familiar occurrence in my life. I had no idea where I would spend the night. Considering I had also lost my bag in all the movement it takes coming to America; I had no bag for my belongings. My property was scattered all over the gravel. I had not seen this coming and today when I reflect, I understand there were influences that pushed her to make this move. I cannot explain why she had a change of heart. I can only tell my story as it unfolded. One thing I know is my story from pain to purpose would not be what it is if it had not been for the pain of that first step. What's clear to me is the pain she inflicted on that day played a major role in my growth, my pursuit of passion and now my ability to accelerate into extraordinary levels.

A Destiny Helper to the Rescue

I remember the moment vividly as I began to pick up my belongings one by one. While I was doing this, through my tears, I could see a car had parked in front of me. My friend then was still yelling and mocking me. I wiped my tears, as the picture of who was coming towards me became clearer. I could see it was the lady I had gone to church with earlier upon my arrival. She inquired, and I poured out my story through the tears. She invited me to spend the night in her room (she rented only a room as she was a student). I remember that night sitting on the corner of her bed, as the room was small. At some point, I fell asleep somewhere in the room with no plan but full of hope for tomorrow. I slept in that small room that night. However the hospitality was so grand because of the mercy shown me. God was in control.

> "*Wherefore, if God so clothe the grass of the field, which today is, and tomorrow is cast into the oven, shall he not much more clothe you, O ye of little faith?*" (Matthew 6:30)

Help for the Journey

The next day I woke up, and word traveled to those that I had made connections with that I was destitute. But God......

Help came from one lady I will never forget to this day. I was offered a room by an angel God sent, the woman whose hair I had done on my arrival to the US. My daughter accidentally found this kind lady's picture as I was writing this book; I didn't even realize I still had this picture. When I saw her picture in 2020, it brought tears to my eyes, and I realized the major role she played in providing me shelter and escaping homelessness in my new location, a land still foreign to me.

This kind helper had just graduated from college and was flying back to her country in Ghana to live permanently. She, however, had a few months left on her lease in the apartment she had been leasing with her roommate. When she heard my story, she offered the room and required no money down. I just had to promise that I would pay the remaining rent monthly till the end of the lease. She left me all her possessions; a mattress, a green chair, some blankets, food in the kitchen, and everything she could not take with her. She even went a step further and ensured that I would not be tormented once she left. She left terms in place with my new roommate which stipulated that only I could stay in her room and in that space for the remaining months. I went to sleep that night with hope. God made a way. Overnight, I had a place to put my head, running water, and yes, electricity. Even at my lowest, I never went so deep as to forget that there was hope, and I had dared to believe. People speak about daring to believe, but I can assure you, at that moment, in that space, I dared to believe and was rewarded. There are times in life where faith meets you in the air. You don't have time to doubt. The only option is to look to the hills and believe. I did and life responded. Another step along the journey was taken.

Life as a Black, Female Foreigner

When I left Zimbabwe, I had no idea the challenges that I would face related to my race, my gender, and my geographical location. I came into America with a strong Zimbabwean accent. I was raised in a culture that was colonized by the British. I was educated under the British system and was very familiar with British English. I remember having scored very highly in my "A" level English literature classes, knowing I was a good student in the English language back home, only to come into the United States of America, start college, and feel as if I knew nothing. It was a rude awakening for me because nobody really tells you about the cultural differences between the different countries when you are planning to migrate. The American way of speaking and writing was a hurdle that saw my grades plummeting dismally. And what's interesting is that everyone assumed that the way I was writing in the British style was wrong, yet all my life I had been taught that that was the right way to do things. This was one of the biggest hurdles I had to face. I had to get remediation during college. It was embarrassing. I had to work hard to understand the different ways of speaking when I spoke to other people. They didn't understand what I was saying because of the different pronunciations of the words. The way Americans use the word "Z" was different from how we used it back in Africa. How you say "the route" is completely different from how we pronounced the word in Zimbabwe, Africa. Communication became a barrier in every single aspect of my life. The pain of trying to be heard and trying to speak sometimes left me silent in situations and in classrooms because they just didn't understand me. At times it became frustrating as you're trying to explain a concept and you're trying to communicate and nobody seems to understand. My accent was thick, rich and robust and was hard for regular people in the American system to understand. My pronunciation, my accent, even the depth of my voice left people bewildered. This was a constant pain that nobody understood.

Additionally, I was female and I was alone transitioning into this new country of mine. I am grateful that at 19 years of age, I was so young and naïve that I did not understand the dangers that were lurking. I would go to my college classes and when they were over, without thinking about it, would cycle back to my home as late as 10:00 in the evening. I even remember passing through some railroad tracks. Today

I realize how dangerous it was, but during that time it never crossed my mind. What was important was the desire I had in me to overcome whatever challenge I encountered fueled by the fire that was burning inside me, and the vision I had for my life. These things left no room for fear. There was never a question of whether I was going to cycle in the dark. There was not even a question in my mind of my safety. What I carried inside of me was far greater than any force outside. I knew there was no option but to press in.

I can recall the many times as a young woman finding her way how I would get propositioned by men in my journeys. I thank God my inner resolve never even considered accepting their propositioning. The answer was always NO! When I look back today, I realized that those instances of proposition could have been the downfall of my life and my destiny. I could have landed in the wrong hands, but I thank God I did not. When I started working, I remember people congregating and speaking to each other about me, my culture, the way I spoke and the way I dressed. Nobody addressed me directly, but I became the source of ridicule and mockery and laughing and disrespect. People can be so bold in putting another person down. They get so caught up in what's wrong with someone else they become insensitive to peoples' feeling and emotions. What they fail to understand is just because you are used to things being done a certain way does not mean that is the only way. What I do know about my journey is that when people looked at me, to them I looked like a museum display, in an unknown, unfamiliar territory. What they missed was the fact that I represented a world they knew nothing about. Wisdom would have had them asking me where I was from, asking me about my culture and about the other world that existed. They could have developed a new determination or fire to venture into an unknown world - in this case Zimbabwe, Africa, perhaps. But unfortunately, the status quo people believe that the life they have is the only life. They wrongly believe that what's unfamiliar is not normal and has no benefit. But what they missed was a person with vision and a destiny who was in their midst at a specific time in a specific season that they could have learned and drawn from to impact their own destiny in the life.

Finally, I remember my life as a foreigner. There was no manual for "when you come into America." In retrospect this could have been a potentially dangerous situation as well. I did not come from a place full of hatred because of the color of your skin. Most people were the same. Today I know that racial issues exist, but I didn't know that when I arrived back then. It could have been dangerous for me to walk into a place that was heavily antiblack and assume that all was well. Yet no one ever schooled me on the areas that you may not be welcome, or that people may not take it lightly if you went into those areas. As I reflect today so many years after, I experience chills to the bone when I remember some of the spaces I went into and the looks I got venturing into those spaces. I went into racially charged places and acted as if business as usual. I had no idea what it meant to be there. I remember people wearing Confederate T-shirts and I had no idea what it meant not knowing the history behind that flag. I know there needs to be more understanding and sympathy for foreigners to help them understand what the social norms are in this country. I am grateful that the hand of God was on my life as I navigated this country as a young, black, African American woman. I am thankful for the Holy Spirit inside me that gave me the understanding of places that I should not have gone and God placing people in my path strategically to help me along the way.

In all of this, I still do vividly remember the pain of trying to understand the culture I had no idea about. The pain of trying to explain who I was, my intentions and my background. It was a big hurdle in that season, this pain of being misunderstood and not understanding the social norms. But I am grateful because during that time what I did was drown myself in educating myself with this new culture. I began to understand how people think and I pulled on those that we knew about the culture. I became an understudy to them to understand what the expectations were. I was learning America, the pain of transition.

Now I have a passion to help people understand the importance of cultural sensitivity to foreigners and this applies to any country in the world. The same should be true when anyone goes to a foreign country, including an American visiting Zimbabwe. Zimbabweans will need to be culturally sensitive too. We complain about discrimination between Blacks and whites, between other people of color and white people, but my question is we need to also understand that within our African American culture there is an element of cultural insensitivity that is just as detrimental and painful to the recipient of this insensitivity.

Chapter 5

A DIFFERENT LENS OF PAIN

As I settled into America, and over the next two years, I established myself in college and worked as a nursing assistant to sustain myself. I was young, hardworking, and alone. My journey to purpose was progressive. Over the years, I would evolve and go through various phases of transformation. Every season of my life was important to mold my character and fuel the fire burning within. The good built my character, and the bad sharpened and prepared me to war.

My life's journey continued as I briefly dated a good friend who, looking back I barely knew, and we soon got married. I was very focused on the destination I had in mind, working two to three jobs and planning where we would be in five years. Unfortunately, I missed the red flags that were all around me and settled for a common life: work, sleep, hangout, and doing the same thing every day over and over again.

After growing up in a life of poverty and adversity, I just wanted someone to love me and protect me. However, I married before I understood relationships, marriage, true love, and above all, my value. As a result, my naïveté and inexperience would be no match for what was on the horizon. My worldview at the time was through rose-colored glasses. Those glasses would take on a different hue as I quickly learned that my husband and I did not have the same drive nor goals. He had his reasons for being present in my life; unfortunately, those reasons were not necessarily with my best interests in mind.

The marriage was riddled with pain on all levels. I have three beautiful children from that marriage, now 17, 15 and 13, all whom I adore. The first years of our marriage were very tough with three babies all just two years apart. We struggled to make ends meet. We ate ramen noodles, canned foods, and took out payday advances. I remember looking for a babysitter. My parents were still in Africa, too far to help. No one in the United States would help me for free and I could not afford to pay for a babysitter. When I reflect on my life and that season of marriage, there were a lot of lessons learned. The beauty is I made it through that season, and we are all still standing.

Although I enjoyed my work as a certified nursing assistant, I had a much grander vision for my life. I needed to go further in college. My third baby, my beloved daughter, would come at the height of living paycheck to paycheck.

There was a future I could still see clearly in my mind; however, the immediate needs of my life and family did not support the vision. Yet the fire burning inside never lost its spark. It burned intensely, waiting for the day I would feed it fuel. Soon my mom caught the vision and came to America, supporting me by gathering up my three babies and returning to Africa to care for them. I remember how hard it was saying goodbye to my seven-month-old. It ripped my heart apart. However, I knew I had to create a better income and life for them long term.

There were many nights I cried for my babies, but I would wipe my tears, wake up, suit up, and fight for our future. I enrolled in an accelerated registered nurse program that took me a year. Upon graduating, I immediately enrolled in a bachelor's degree program in nursing. During this period, I would speak to my children by phone, though it was not enough. My only comfort was the consuming fire burning inside my heart that demanded I press on and create permanent emancipation for my family. Poverty had to be eliminated from our lineage, and there was no time to nurse my feelings. I worked hard and sent money home frequently. US dollars went a long way in Zimbabwe. The children were showered with their grandparents' attention, multiple maids, and caregivers in Africa. They even had a chauffeur to drive them to school and back.

Though the marriage was a disappointment, we did produce three beautiful, children; two daughters and a son. My children light up my world and are a source of continuous joy. In all my chasing, what continues to pull me to press in are my children. They push me to want to be better and bolder. I wake up fighting because I understand that I am also fighting for their life and future.

My babies have had their own experiences surviving the single mom household; however, they too have a light that shines so bright each day. I am so proud to be their mom. My ex-husband and I were married for 10 years, and we were leading separate lives for the bulk of that time. In that decade I could not be the highest version of myself. I wanted more out of life, but the marriage did not honor this need. The fire inside me that brought me to the United States started to dwindle. There was just nothing in the relationship for me, no light, no flame, no passion. I gained weight, became clinically depressed, developed hypertension, and struggled to breathe, later being diagnosed with asthma. Eventually we would drift off into separate lives while still married. The divorce was merely a formality to something that was already done.

The Resilience of Children

Deciding to move and reclaim your life while you are breaking a family apart is the hardest decision any woman should have to make. While contemplating divorce and going through the motions of the marriage relationship, I stumbled into a conversation with a close friend and they asked if I was doing the children a favor or a disfavor by the example of marriage and family we were displaying in front of them. I remember how I felt during this season. I never smiled. There was nothing but gloom in my world. Every day I went through the motions of life, I knew something was off and there was no doubt I was unhappy.

This period of my life reminds me that we need to be careful not to become comfortable with pain. Even though I knew it felt bad, even though I knew something was off, the more I sat in this comatose state the more tolerance I developed. It was as if I was in deep sleep. This was the person my children got to see every day. Though it was hard to move forward and start anew, I decided my children deserved a better life. My children deserved to smile large genuine smiles. The need to win my children's smiles and pass on a different life better that what they had, drove me out of my slumber. When we finally broke the news to the world that we were moving forward with the divorce, this was a hard pill to swallow for the children and family. I had to believe in my decision and stand strong and support my children through the heartache of being between two homes. They coped as best they could. They were innocent and only knew what they saw. I continued to support them as best as I could, but the hardest part of the divorce was them being in the middle. They were repeatedly in the middle of a never-ending battle and dispute based on someone else's opinion.

I believe when people go their separate ways, they should try to maintain normal conduct and treat each other with dignity for the benefit of the children. I can truly say I would have loved for my children

42

to not have gone through half of what they went through; however such is life. Today I am encouraged as I am striving to shower them with love, empower them with purpose and give them permission to be children and to grow and mature at their own organic pace. I have learnt in everything to love them and fight for them. There were endless battles it seemed I fought over the years to defend my children. Some battles left battle scars on me as a person. However, if I had to do it again, I would fight every battle for my children again, I would sound the alarm each time no matter what I faced because they are innocent. Today my children are thriving. They too are learning to turn pain to purpose. My children have a fire that is burning, not unlike their mother. They have resilience, a heart for the disadvantaged, the forgotten and the lost. My children are moving forward into the future united and ready to take on the world. We have a joint fire that burns with purpose, born out of a life riddled with adversity. This is indeed our life from pain to purpose.

The Root of Fractured Intimate Relationships

After the divorce, I found myself in a vicious cycle of bad love relationships. For years after my divorce, I was involved in relationships where I was emotionally, mentally and verbally abused. These relationships were the definition of pain. It is amazing to me how we end up in relationships that disempower us and tear us down, yet we still stay. Even as a highly intelligent woman, I subjected myself to these abusive relationships repeatedly.

The nature of my relationships with men was born from how I was introduced to love as a teenager back home. I remember that first person who defined how I would view future relationships as if it was yesterday. I met this person in a remote town while working. He was a handsome guy, well-educated and he showed interest in me at the tender age of 16. I was just so young. When I look back, he was not 100% invested, he was just showing interest and I showed interest back, so he pursued. I would be the one to call this guy on the phone. If I did not call, he never looked for me. But when I called him, he answered the phone and we spoke for the time. Something in me thought that meant he was interested. So you see, I started at a young age putting in the work in relationships even when the other party did not reciprocate. They gave me very little attention, yet I gave so much. I was OK with that, then. When it was time for him to come to the city, he promised that we would meet. I remember going to the location a day before I was supposed to meet him. I was sitting in my mother's car and as life would have it, he happened to pass by. He was with one of his friends who happened to be an ex-girlfriend's sister. I remember coming out of the car and I didn't even think about it, looking basic, but I stopped him and inquired if we were still meeting tomorrow. He looked me straight in the eyes and said yes, we are meeting tomorrow.

The next day I woke up, got dressed and went to meet him at the place. I got there super early and happily waited. He never came. I must have waited half the afternoon; he had promised to be there and so I waited. It must have been about a 6-hour wait, maybe even more. This was my introduction to the world of relationships. Rejection was the calling card. I still couldn't believe a person could look you straight in your face and lie saying they will be there and they do not come. This was my earliest experience with disappointment in relationships. As the years would go by, he continued to waste my time, and I let him. He would be present in my life yet still unavailable. Eventually after I came to America, he tried to reconnect on a very superficial level until one day I decided enough was enough. But this poor start had already set the stage for how I would view relationships.

As women we do not realize that how we let other people treat us slowly takes away our power. Slowly it affects our future relationships like a cancer. There should never be a day as a woman you stand for less than or accept being treated in a way that does not feel good to you. Allowing someone to reject and disappoint you disempowers and destroys your potential destiny and your perspective on future relationships. Today you need to know who you are, and you need to live your life knowing your value. When people come into your space and do not level up to your value, you need to have the peace and self-respect to politely escort them out of your life. Your time is valuable, and you deserve the full solution of love and nothing less. My experience may help those who are entertaining time wasters who are not pouring the attention and appreciation you deserve. Always know - you have so much value, you matter, and there is an amazing life that awaits you.

Subsequent Relationships

The relationships I found myself in after the divorce, one after another, did not bring anything different, they brought with them only more rejection and ridicule. It seems as if they came around knowing that they could come and play around my heart, and not give me the full love that I know I was created to enjoy. It took a while for me to realize that they were not who I needed in my life. I had to learn that a relationship should not cause pain, anguish or wonder if somebody wants to be with you. There is nothing perplexing about love, but there is something clear about a person who has only good intentions to be with you. One should want to be with you, and love being with you. I was in relationships where people hated me. I mean you could visibly see the hate on a person's face, and I sat there and let the person be in my space. It was my space, but I let them infuse toxic vibes and energy into my space. This eventually seeped into my being and the world around me. I've had men speak to me as if I was beneath them. Because I didn't know who I was, they could speak to me any kind of way. Because I didn't really love myself, this opened the door for disrespect and abuse.

Seeing Through New Eyes

While connected to these men, I did not realize that the relationships were intentionally keeping me from realizing my true potential. Looking back, I was belittled and mocked by the same people who were supposed to "love me." What is love, right? I share this journey because as my power was stripped yet again, I experienced the all too familiar feelings of rejection and worthlessness.

After each attempt for a meaningful relationship, I would hit rock bottom. I found myself so disempowered that it began to permeate into every area of my life. I kept saying to myself, "I am made for more." The more I said this, the more I started to believe. Eventually that thought began to germinate. Then pure revelation came... *Melody, you were made for more and God loves you.*

I didn't need a man's love, but I had a father in heaven that loved me so well. My father in Heaven put me on this earth, fully equipped for everything, bursting with purpose and assignment for this life. I rose from the place of rejection, bad relationships and chronic poverty. I was bursting out of being spoken to any kind of way. I rose and I declared war upon the squatters that had come to squat in my life, hogging my inbox. These men found the time to disappear for months on end and then would suddenly appear, still thinking I was in that same space. I sent the squatters packing, I made sure they understood who I was and how valuable I was and how they were no longer welcome to pitch their tents and bring their contamination near me. It was no longer ok to bring their toxic, broken, childlike ways near me. I rose up to understand that I was the daughter of a King. I understood that God had such amazing plans for me and that there was a pure and perfected love that God had for me. I began to love myself and by loving myself I began to understand the love that I now demanded for me. It was no longer hard to live the single life; being single was a privilege as I waited for real love.

In hindsight, I understood that these relationships created confusion and a smokescreen that concealed the destiny that God had for me. I was meant to fight for the underdog, the weak woman, the abused woman. However, if I was fighting the same evils I allowed into my own life, I could never come out to be the one fighting against those relationships. So, I had to go through those relationships and take steps to build myself up in order to be able to fight and advocate for other women. In all of this, I learned my power came from my relationship with God. Through him I found the power to get myself free from these toxic relationships. Yet even after the relationships were long gone, the residue from their toxicity remained. As I rose from the ashes, I learnt to turn the pain from those feelings of rejection, pain, ridicule, mocking and abuse into passion. This newfound passion gave me the ability and fire to reach out and help other women rise from their pain. I learnt to bring a message of hope and fire breathing passion to women ready to chase purpose in their Kingdom assignment and walk into my destiny. It was then I realized I was born for such a time as this!

Pointed to Destiny

So, the journey to my destiny began as I started to research the effects of abusive relationships. I would soon realize I had been robbed of my happiness, my joy, my courage, and my life. When the effects of these toxic relationships are apparent, they can greatly alter your mindset, and your other relationships. We need to understand that when we allow people to speak negatively about us or our lives, we give up our power, our purpose, and our destiny. Domination by another human being chokes out what God has planned for your life. The solution: **RUN** from any form of domination.

Once I ran from these limiting relationships, the beginning of uncovering my true value began. I opened myself to the undeniable fact that I was loved, bought with a price, and if a mortal man did not have the capacity to love me, then I had a Father in heaven who loved me unconditionally. When the light and the love of God entered my whole being, all dark areas of my life began to fall off, including those people and things that did not serve me. I became consumed with this new revelation, and every day I sharpened my understanding of my value. As my perception grew from seed to a watered plant, I began to run, and run hard; away from those things that I was overcoming. From the dim light inside me grew a slow and steady flame. It may not have been gigantic, but it was strong. I began to rise from paralyzing fear to fire-breathing purpose. Purpose to speak on behalf of the rejected, disempowered, mocked, and cast away. The power of a clear vision transformed who I was, the people I allowed into my space, and the people I spent my life serving. One day, I was an abused woman, and the next day, I was a woman of resilience.

Finding the Love of God

Today, I understand that one's intelligence does not factor into the snare of an abuser. One of those bad relationships I found myself in involved intimate partner abuse. The effects of intimate partner abuse deposited in me a sensitivity towards those affected and afflicted by this danger. I received the revelation that the pain being inflicted on me had nothing to do with me, but it had everything to do with the person that was inflicting the pain. I realized that I was worth more than what they said I was, and God loved me before the foundation of the earth. The change in my perception became the springboard that walked me into a different dimension and made me a different person. I overcame that pain, and emerged a person with compassion, a person who understands that same type of pain. I stand on my life experiences as a champion against that same pain. I became a person that can minister and mentor those who have experienced that pain. My greatest life experiences have given me the advantage to enter the trenches with those still stuck and assist them back to safety, pointing out the essential players and helpers along the way. The greatest battle against these attacks starts in the mind, in your own perception. You must know who you are, and what you possess. If you can develop this perception, no matter what you have gone through, you can turn your pain into fuel and your new mindset will win the war for you.

Perception moved me into a different way of doing things. It moved me to understand my true value and worth. Perception made me stronger than the pain.

Paradigm Shift

To experience personal transformation from the old self, one must leave old habits and patterns and develop and sustain new ones. The new habits must align with the expected end goal. When I began to value myself, I knew I was enough. I unmasked the lies and strategies of the enemy that had followed me since that first encounter at 16. I also realized how strategic and dare I say precious adversity would be to my overall growth and capacity. My new perception of myself and reality made room for new goals and a new mindset. I developed new habits and reinvented myself mentally, emotionally, and physically. I began to model the patterns of the people that I knew and looked up to. I was able to change my paradigm. As I began to exercise healthy habits, I transformed into the highest version of myself. I tapped into my power. I discovered the power that had lain dormant all this time. My power came from my painful life experiences, the scars that remained and the fire that stilled burned deep inside. When all three collided, they produced a slow and steady pace and flame. This transformation created an atmosphere that now appreciates the small things in life because you have been on the other side.

My own victory over relationship abuse and pain created in me a burden for other women that were abused mentally and physically. I began to minister to them and help them become better versions of themselves in their families, careers, and love.

Chapter 6

BIRTH OF THE PAIN TO PURPOSE BRAND

My awakening from the abuse, ridicule and mocking, along with the birth of a passion to help women in pain was the beginning of the pain to purpose brand and my journey as a pain to purpose accelerator. My assignment is to help women understand that hidden within their pain is dynamite power. When the pressure breaks, a right perception will ignite a spark. The spark becomes the fire, and this fire is deposited during the painful experiences. When you find your voice and power, eventually you will rise and walk on purpose. Women of purpose will live a life impacting their families, their community, the nation, and the world.

Most of us are gifted people who are supposed to impact the world. The devil has used pain to keep us down, but the revelation that your pain is your ministry is a game changer. Your purpose will move you to a place of power, position, authority, and impact. Welcome to your time of transformation!!

Power

Purpose is a journey; it is the path that takes us to finding out who we are and why we exist. We chase purpose and our earthly assignment until the day we take our last breath. Once you know your purpose, you can then receive the power to get the assignment done. Power is a byproduct when one moves from the source of pain. You give it a name, and you know what type of pain and affliction followed you and take authority over it, thereby changing our perception towards the pain. We do not despise the pain. Instead, we draw out its valuable lessons. We take inventory of the areas we developed strength in and move into our next season standing on these strengths. Life's most challenging experiences are the vehicle to our destiny. The breakthrough from pain to purpose for me lies heavily in my ability to switch my mindset from pain to focusing on the journey. The steps I take daily are deposits into each season and my ultimate transformation A change in your paradigm and mindset produces growth and harnesses breakthrough power. Perpetual pain stretches our character, creating endurance and resilience. The result of these new traits allows one to reach new levels of power in life, business, and relationships.

During my experiences, I leaned on the story of David and Goliath in the Bible. I have used key life principles from this story to inform my own. Young David was in the wilderness fighting lions and bears, but no one was ever there with him as he was fighting. But we know one thing, there was a young boy in the wilderness with a slingshot. And so it is in my life. I may not have physically killed a live bear, but in my time, I have had to kill the bear of generational patterns. There had to have been an element of fight and an element of fear when David was fighting and conquering in the wilderness. But what made David overcome and defeat the bear and the lion was the urgency of fighting for his life. This same fight was perfected the day David walked onto the battlefield to confront the uncircumcised Philistine Goliath. Pain is the preparation that allows us to live an overcoming life of power, power over every obstacle and situation. Pain is our preparation in the wilderness. David had been through the pain, he had been stretched, he had been injured, he had seen so much adversity that this situation was small. The wilderness season prepared young David to rise in boldness. He picked up his slingshot with razor sharp focus, and with one shot, he defeated the Philistine.

Transformation

My transformation started the day I understood who I was and what I was called to do. This new perception paved the way for forward movement. This was the spark that produced power to walk and momentum to stay every day.

I come from Zimbabwe, Africa. I have been through great hardship along my journey. I've shared with you the pain I endured from bullying by school children as a child into adulthood where I experienced intimate partner abuse. But my path required me to align myself with people who had overcome and people that were living the life that God intended for me to live. So, by changing my patterns, I was able to instinctively start walking in power. Each change in my paradigm became a solid power habit.

As I reached back to other women in the low place, sharing my story and my process, my true power emerged. I shared how I overcame the pain and today I live to tell the story. Over time, this has become a checks and balance system, keeping me liberated, strengthening my process, and changing the lives of women worldwide. Power comes as a result of a commitment to follow healthy patterns for your life that lead to empowerment.

Under the Canopy of Stars

As you can see, I didn't just wake up walking passionately on purpose. My story unfolded over time; from one of poverty, pain, and ridicule to abundance, hope, faith, and purpose.

Let me take you back to Africa for just a moment to remember that young girl with a dream. I recall sitting outside on one of the many nights with my five siblings, parents, and relatives around a fire, cooking a hot dinner. As I looked up into the beautiful African sky, I saw a blanket of beautiful stars. Growing up, my parents went out of their way to provide shelter to relatives, those in need, and at one time even providing shelter for a homeless child. My parents' hospitality and compassion were never based on our financial state. They helped those in need all year round. We were outside because our electricity had been turned off; this was one of those times where there were no lights for months. We cooked outside, heated water for bathing, made tea as a nightcap, all on a fire. This fire we sat around, as it burned bright, enabled us to continue to live life from its natural source. I remember many nights sitting and looking into the flames and enjoying the heat. You could see our faces, our smiles, and our worries through the flames. When you looked up into the African sky, it was covered with a blanket of stars, shining so bright, some brighter than others. At times you could see what we called a shooting star shoot out fast and reposition itself in the sky. And then there was the moon that had the final say for the night providing light.

It would be times like these that I would see beyond our problems. I looked at the stars and knew there were no limits to my future if I only believed. The fire that burned within me needed to be fed with firewood, paper at times, or just a gentle breath would be enough to keep the flame alive. These times of reflection around the fire would stoke the passion within my soul, a passion to excel and beat the odds of limitation forever. I would be the first in my generation to dare to dream, to break generational curses, pursue my faith, and conquer new territories. I believed; therefore, I lived a full life, walking straight into my future with God as my anchor and Jesus as my savior.

Pain or repetitive patterns of pain may be a problem in your life. However, where there is passion, there is no limitation. Bone chilling winter poverty and desert dry summer adversity could not dim the light in me or the raging fire that burned. I was consumed with pursuing a future like no other. I became blind to adversity and stepped over every Pharaoh, Goliath, and Red Sea with determination and resolve. I stood tall by every Jericho wall in faith.

There was a force and a power greater than me. I would and still do, watch every wall fold, then crush to pieces and bow to the name Jesus. Passion was the vehicle that overcame every obstacle as I journeyed into the promised land of the United States of America. Passion made me rise.

Chapter 7

IT'S A NEW SEASON

Reading my journey and thinking about your own, you may ask yourself how I ended up in these abusive relationships. I would like to step back a minute and revisit that time, not to gain sympathy, but to tie it into how I transitioned from pain to purpose. Abuse is subtle, and it creeps in. Abusers persuade their victims under false pretenses and exaggerated kindness. As I stated above, intelligence does not exempt you from these predators, as they are skillful hunters that prey on women with insecurities and low self-esteem. Yes, I was that woman!

Following a failed marriage which blessed me with three beautiful children, I endeavored to move into a new life. Unfortunately, there was residue due to previously inflicted emotional damage that existed in me at that time. I found myself continuously and repeatedly in the hands of manipulative, abusive, and narcissistic men. One incident stuck out to me where I visited a lover to surprise him. Unsuspecting and in "love" with this man, I was soon shown how unwelcome I was within the city limits. I found out this man had a lover in that city, and I was not the priority. This was a shocking revelation I do not wish any woman should ever experience. I stood and watched as my bags were thrown out of the house and landed on the dirt. I stood there as someone devalued me and made me feel worthless. In that moment, I met a different person than I had known. All I wanted was to be back home in my warm house, with my family, my loving children, and friends.

I was far from home and would face the reality that there was more for me in this life than to be at the mercy of some ruthless, bully that had no identity. That night, a kind stranger would stand by my side, help me to the airport, and place me on an airplane to return home. As the plane ascended into the air, I would cry for seven hours. When I stopped crying, I would fall asleep, only to wake up to my reality and start crying again.

Sustaining Power

I love how life has a way of depositing what we need for the future through experiences. It is through these repeated abusive experiences that I would find my purpose in helping women overcome abuse, overcome the residue of abuse, and to live a life full of passion as the highest version of themselves. I wake up with determination to help women see their value, know their value, and step into their value. It's important to say yes to yourself and accept the good life, good relationships, and the blessings that come from God. As I hit rock bottom on the plane that night flying back home, this vicious man would send word to everyone I knew that I was confused and straight crazy But that's ok because here we are now, the proof is in the pudding. These uncomfortable experiences agitated my status quo and forced me to change my position. Today, because of my pain, I help women solve the same issues I encountered using the tools I employed to overcome abusive patterns. The pain points I overcame gave me tools that I share with those in the trenches to help dig them to safety and stay in the higher life.

Purpose

Our pursuit in life should lead us to our passion. Passion is the beginning of a life of service in the thing that fuels you, and this gives breath to your being. You find fulfillment in serving the world and humanity. What you do no longer feels like work, it becomes service. You join the privileged few who have found their purpose helping humanity for the greater good. When you are walking in purpose, you realize new strengths. When we live in a place of strength and power, we are operating in the highest version of ourselves. Purpose is not a destination that we strive to achieve. Purpose is the place that we get to when we finally find the reason we were born, the reason we live, and the reason that we are here. Purpose is knowing your assignment on this earth, which was predestined at conception. When we finally know this, we begin living, walking, and breathing in a place of purpose.

Perspective

Our whole life story is a scroll slowly written leading to your purpose. The difference is some may never wake up to realize they have the power to actively engage in their life story. Understanding the why of your existence breaks open a new world of service to the world. My encouragement it to take a moment and look at your life story from birth to present. What stands out in your upbringing, what battles have you had to fight, what is God calling you to do now. I can assure you there is a link from childhood to today of your experiences and your purpose. All that is needed is clarity of purpose. Clarity makes the journey easier and you learn to not resist the plan God has for you.

Parents of Faith

I am thankful to my parents for they have always had the revelation that I was chasing something greater than myself. They never tried to stop me; they would always step out of the way or make room for me to explore. They enlarged my mental territory and moved people out of my way.

I completed my nursing program after four years; however, I needed a few thousand dollars to fly my three children home and bring my parents to the US. Heavily loaded with student loans, I cashed in the 401k I had acquired with my employer and bought tickets for them all. I had to have my babies, and I wanted my parents to benefit from the sacrifices they had made for me and the children. So after four long years, my children were on US soil with me again, and the journey continued.

Prior to this reunion, the pain of not being a mother in this season was heartbreaking. My youngest left for Africa at seven months. My brave daughter had left when she was still sitting on my lap, and my son who was so close to me was miles away. I could not hear my older daughter's laughter for four solid years. But I endured this waiting period, because of the greater that awaited me on the other side. The greater gave me the strength to put one foot in front of the other every single day. The fire that burned inside urged me to keep going.

I conquered education, depression, and weight gain. I worked with a psychologist and a personal trainer, I learned to shift my current paradigm to a new paradigm that aligned with positive moves and experiences. And of course as noted above, the marriage fell apart during this time. It could not withstand the pressure and the work that destiny required based on my predestined purpose.

If you asked me why we divorced a few years back, the reason for the divorce would have been different. Today, I have clarity that the marriage had no chance because we were chasing different things. I had a fire and was chasing vision, passion, and purpose, while the other party was content and had arrived. I cannot and could not afford to be content because behind me was a tribe and community that needed support and lifting. Every meal I ate, all the luxuries we had, I would sit wondering about my family in Zimbabwe. What about my community and my country?

The journey to purpose is never one you do alone. We have people who support us and make it possible to be who we are called to be. We need to treasure the relationships around us. We may not always agree, however the value of the support is priceless. Developing an attitude of gratitude and respect for loved ones, friends and people that help us along the way is important and a magnet to greater levels of blessing.

Special Son, Special Blessing

When I married, I was only 21 – just two years after my arrival in the US. The marriage was a story of wins, triumphs, and ultimately many regrets. Out of this marriage, I was blessed with two daughters and a son. I like to call my son special, because he is special. My son was born early and had a low birth weight. He progressed well until he took too long to speak words and make conversation. I remember before I set out to get an official diagnosis from his doctors, as a mom, I sensed what they would tell me. He started his early years in Zimbabwe.

My mother was gracious enough to fly to Zimbabwe with my children to give me a fair chance of completing my associate degree in nursing. I have fought the good fight to obtain an education amid raising children as a single mom. I have had to wage war for my education and conquer great armies of trials and tribulation. I am grateful today for my mother's labor of love. I remember the day she left with the children. I understand the sacrifices made by many in my journey. They were those who would let me stand on their shoulders and are a big part of where I am today. Along the way were the destiny helpers who helped me carry the weight.

When my son returned to the United States, he had received a diagnosis of autism in Zimbabwe and was attending a special school with children who were just like him. As a mother, it was a scary road with so many uncertainties. I found very little help and information including how to care for and raise a son with autism. Due to my middle-income status, I could not obtain disability benefits for him or state assistance. My work insurance did not cover a diagnosis of autism, so I paid for services out of my pocket and networked with other moms. Yes, at times I thought about returning to Zimbabwe. Twice I tried to relocate geographically to Canada, and the United Kingdom, because their systems were better setup to help my son.

I had many challenges while he was growing up. I was a single mom, working full time, and yes, I continued with school and eventually completed my master's degree. There were so many tears, and so many times I blamed myself for my son's condition. My breakthrough came when I learned to contend on behalf of my son, to pray, to intercede, to cry, to go before the altar of God and cry out in the spirit to save my son. I am reminded of the story of Hagar and God's response to Ishmael's cry. I cried as a mother on behalf of my son and God heard the prayer.

"And God heard the voice of the lad; and the angel of God called to Hagar out of heaven, and said unto her, What aileth thee, Hagar? fear not; for God hath heard the voice of the lad where he is."(Genesis 21:17 KJV).

I would cry out, "Father, save my son. You gave him to me with a purpose, I give him to you; but Father, please save him." The cry of a desperate mom even God cannot ignore.

Today I am so grateful that I found peace and that my son is able to care for himself, speaks well, and only needs gentle guidance. But the truth is, it was all the hand of God and his mercy. My ultimate victory with my son came when I accepted him as God had created him. He carefully delivered him to me to care for him. I rested in knowing my role was to be present in his life, guide him, and love him unconditionally. My son can do so many amazing things. He can complete a puzzle in very little time with no assistance. He has great discernment and only feels comfortable with gentle souls. He is very loving and caring. He loves to draw and paint. Every day I discover new talents about him. It all began when I accepted him as he was and stopped placing limits on him, based on society norms; limits we often put on ourselves and others when we believe things are out of our control.

My son has taught me unconditional love, patience, surrender, and full trust in God. His life has brought me closer to God because I realize he is a child of God and God has kept him. My special son is a gift, and my hope is to inspire other women with children with special needs that our children need us. More importantly, our special children need us.

I believe my son's destiny is bright. His life story taught me to war, to war on his behalf and fight like a bear for his welfare. I have a passion to help those disadvantaged and afflicted. I will continue to follow the fire that burns inside. His story will give other families hope to the possibility of a quality life, no matter the label society has placed on you. The fire of

God can and will burn through any limitation. It will not delay but give divine speed. I have seen this in my son's life. When they said he would not talk, he freely converses today. Let the fire of hope continue to burn.

My mission is to inspire hope into your life for the things we may feel we are unable to handle. Hope to understand that all things are working for your good and that we serve a God of the impossible where miracles still do happen. It's important to never lose hope, trust God and live an abundant life through Jesus Christ of Nazareth, the son of God.

Many Lessons

It took me awhile to realize that my dream from Zimbabwe to the world would teach me a lot of lessons. I was in the school of life and every day had its challenges. The important lesson is that all our past experiences have prepared us for our challenges in the present and future. They have deposited in us the tools needed to face life every day. My life and my process gave me patience, endurance, power, life, humility, silent strength, and many more gifts. When we face situations that seem greater than us, we need to take a moment and take inventory. We need to ask what is going on and develop a strategy to navigate the new season. We must show up consistently with a set of behaviors that reflect where we are going and take each day and season as it comes. The fire that burns deep in my soul has been chasing purpose from Zimbabwe to the world, and it will not stop now.

One-Person Gateway

When I was a child, I just knew I was going somewhere, some place far. As I grew up as a young girl in Zimbabwe, Africa, there was an underlying current I could feel. This current was flowing in my life and pointing me into a future I knew very little about, yet it was real. In my life, I walk fearlessly and believe in a power greater than me. I trusted the plans that God had for my life and walked with zero doubt. My decision to come to America began as an individual effort to relocate and to eradicate poverty in my family. I was driven to go to a faraway place and return with newfound hidden treasures that would elevate my family, community, and end generational poverty forever. The quest to end poverty is what I thought was driving me at that time, as I braved into a foreign country at the age of 19. I arrived young and green, ready to learn, listening and transitioning into my new life. A year later, my older sister would join me in the US, and soon our younger sister would join us both as well. I had my three children. My younger sister would also have a daughter. My parents would migrate too and establish themselves as residents. My older brother migrated to South Africa and has three beautiful children, two boys and a daughter. My other older brother remains in Harare, Zimbabwe, married with two daughters, holding down the fort of our family home.

What I know today is what seemed like an innocent decision towards migrating to the United States of America at the age of 19, was not that simple. There was a flame that had been burning low, ignited by years of pictures, imprints, and associations pointing towards a distant land. This slow burning flame was feeding on decisions that aligned with my life purpose. Year by year, through adversity, every conquered season fed the fire, and the flames began to gain strength. I began to walk towards my destiny and the reason I was born. I was just a vessel that paved the way for a whole generational shift in my family. Today, my sisters are well educated. One is a Doctor of Osteopathic Medicine with an internal medicine focus, and my younger sister is an adult nurse practitioner working with the vulnerable and forgotten of our society. They both are making an impact in their spheres of influence. One person walked into the United States of America over 20 years ago with a handful of clothes and lost luggage in Germany, but today, the legacy includes five second-generation children, two sisters and two parents, all living the American Dream. To the naked eye, I arrived in the United States alone; however, I can tell you without a shadow of doubt, I was not alone. I arrived with a flame burning inside and a mighty omnipotent ever-present source, feeding the flame and armed with the power to conquer. It is in Him I live.

The fire that is burning inside me will not stop seeking to create better opportunities for family, friends, children, women, men, and the people of our world in this generation. Today, the fire burning inside has a burden to end poverty, intimate partner abuse, domestic violence, rejection, ridicule, mocking, bullying, racial and gender bias, and all things related to injustice. The fire is burning, the flames are growing, and I am walking in the fire as it points to my next assignment.

Conclusion

THE BURDEN FOR MY PEOPLE

llow me to share with you what is the current burden for my people of Zimbabwe. We are brothers and sisters and spread all over the world. Our new title now is the Diaspora, meaning "the dispersion of any people from their original homeland" (Google definition). The comforting nature of our relationship in a foreign land as Zimbabweans is that when we meet, it doesn't matter what part of Zimbabwe we are from, we are brothers and sisters. In the past, we spent our leisure time together reminiscing about our home and how we miss our land. However, this is a new era. I am experiencing an awakening as I realize women and children don't just need our memories, but our resources and capacity. Our diaspora is well educated in first world countries and now constitute a new intellectual reservoir for our nation and for Africa. It is an important time now to do business in Zimbabwe.

In the different parts of the world where we find ourselves, the people of Zimbabwe represent a new era of influence with unique capacity. It is our business to be constantly building the capacity of our people and our home. We are privileged with knowledgeable entrepreneurs and knowledgeable intellectuals who can explain the processes that we may not understand. The African Diaspora has great wealth of knowledge in educating each other in the different areas of business and humanitarian work as we partner together.

We have a rich mix of qualifications, life experiences, solid beliefs, faith in God, business expertise, and pain that we share and have overcome. Grit has been forged in us as a byproduct of the challenges we have faced in foreign lands scattered across the globe. In addition to who we are collectively, the Zimbabwean Diaspora carries personal value, having defeated myriad adversity and marginalization in the countries we reside. The GAME CHANGER is that we have created worldwide solutions with Zimbabwean solution providers. We are now converging to work together and are beginning to have the conversation, where the questions are asked, and the answer is given by a fellow Zimbabwean sister or brother. The Zimbabwean Diaspora left the country in search of a better life, chasing the fire that burned inside their soul. In this season, those fires are all burning towards our motherland Zimbabwe.

As I move towards the fire, I am fully persuaded that the conversation now flowing for us to advance into different levels of business and different spheres of influences in business is gathering momentum. Our country is rich with natural resources, herbs, plants, and intellectual capacity. Yes, we can do business. This is possible. We are a multifaceted and multitalented people. We are knowledge and solutions, and above all, we have a strong foundation and belief in the God that we serve. A country whose worship is electrifying.

Allow me to draw a lesson from Nehemiah and his rebuilding of the wall. When Nehemiah inquired from one of his brothers and some other men who had come from Judah about the Jewish remnant that had survived the exile, and also about Jerusalem, he was told

> "The wall of Jerusalem is broken down, and its gates have been burned with fire. When I heard these things, I sat down and wept. For some days, I mourned, fasted, and prayed before the God of heaven". (Nehemiah 1:3-4)

Though this news greatly troubled Nehemiah, he knew he had to rise up to help his people. Using his personal influence and supported by his God, Nehemiah was instrumental in the rebuilding of the wall around Jerusalem, systematically, section by section, piece by piece. He was the vessel of honor and the platform God used that would weave together all the components of the walls of Jerusalem. The fire inside Nehemiah burned hot and he walked in the direction of the fire until the project was finished. His mind was set. He would rebuild the walls of Jerusalem, no matter the obstacles.

Like Nehemiah, we each have had a moment where we were steered into action going beyond any obstacles. Like Nehemiah, we have cried out all the way to distant countries. In this season, the Zimbabwean Diaspora women are called to be a part of a remnant of women with a unique mindset, determined to come together and collectively unite and share solutions.

Nehemiah was the platform then and help and resources came. Now, I believe it is our skills and intellect that are the platform. It is time to contribute to rebuilding the walls of influence and expertise that is inside of us so that collectively we will see acceleration and elevation.

From Zimbabwe to the World - No Limits to God (UK, SA, Dubai)

And so, the fire burns. When I came into the United States of America, I was excited to come and live the American Dream. I have chronicled my journey through pain, adversity, rejection, abuse, stigmatization, and the discovery of purpose through pain. I detailed my fight for victory over every barrier, abuse, and adversity. I transitioned to a story of overcoming, victory, and triumph. My journey to the United States was to equip and ignite me for my next assignment towards fulfilling my destiny. After 20 years matriculating through the United States of America's school of life, I moved forward with a master's degree in nursing, an associate's degree in Christian Ministry, and multiple certifications, I stand today simply as a child of God, full of love, driven by my purpose, and ready to change the world. All these degrees and certifications do not define who I am, however, I am grateful for what higher education has afforded me and my family.

Above all, the school of life has seen me through the highs and the lows. One thing that has been constant in my journey, is that in the low places, Jesus powered me through to higher ground. In the storm, Jesus gave me the peace that surpasses all understanding.

And that peace provided me a new worldview with no limits. In 2019 I became the cofounder of a women's organization' dedicated to helping women live abundantly blessed lives, graced with an inaugural conference that brought women together for the greater good.

And so, the fire burns...

By divine intervention, I was invited to speak at an inaugural Zimbabwe Women Do Dubai Conference 2020, organized by Dr. Abigail Magwenzi, the Commander in Chief of the Red Lipstick Revolution. Dr. Magwenzi is a woman of great faith, tenacity, and resolve, dear to my heart for her dedication to the women of this generation. One day before my departure to Dubai, I had to cancel due to emergent health issues. Coincidentally, this happened one week before COVID-19 would bring the world to a standstill. I became sick a day before I was to fly out to Dubai. I may not have made it on that flight to Dubai, but best believe the fire was and will continue to burn. The world's standstill became an opportunity to pivot, regroup, and perfect my message. All roads from 2020 point to the second Zimbabwe Women Do Dubai 2021, a true testament to the power of vision by Dr. Magwenzi.

Now in 2021 I have again received an invitation to speak on the Zimbabwe Women Do Dubai 2021 stage and as heaven would have it, I will be speaking on how Pain is a Purpose Accelerator. I stand in a full circle moment and a testimony of how God orders our steps to bring a message of hope in season. And so, the fire burns...

In This Season

Today my feet are turned towards Zimbabwe to uplift and help in the work to eradicate poverty, gender bias of women, children, the girl child, prejudice, racism, intimate partner abuse, and domestic violence. It is time to build a generation of women, men, and children that will work to rebuild the nation, one relationship and business transaction at a time. The fire is burning, and all roads point to Zimbabwe, providing resources and mindset training to overcome the ruins left by decades of poverty. Poverty may be defeated, but the mind needs to be delivered from limitation. It can and will be done. Zimbabwean women, children, and men will rise.

And so, the fire burns...

Pain to Purpose

In August 2019 I met my business and life coach. I believe God places people in your life to be destiny helpers that move you to fulfill your destiny. The first day I spoke to my coach, my eyes were opened to endless possibilities. Answering the call to continue in my quest to serve the world, I believe I was divinely connected to my coach. When I started working with her, the goal was to find my highest skills from my soft skills and my hard skills to understand my area of expertise. As I began to work on my gifts, talents, and skills, it became apparent I was consistently helping women overcome pain and move into purpose. I have always gravitated to those in pain and been a master motivator, helping them stand on their pain and use their pain as fuel in all areas of their lives. Then my coach helped me to package my gifts and provided me with a blueprint to follow. Today, I wake up able to help women stand on their pain, turning their pain to fuel, to live powerfully in life, leadership, love, relationships, and business. When a woman wins over pain, she is unstoppable, and this filters to all areas of her life. Mentorship and coaching are an important ingredients in moving into your next level. There is power in following behind those that have already been there to show you the how, why and when of your pursuits. We are ever learning, and this is an important part of breaking through limits.

From Zimbabwe, Africa to the World, LET IT BURN!

www.ingramcontent.com/pod-product-compliance
Lightning Source LLC
Chambersburg PA
CBHW031524270326
41930CB00006B/514